ASADO
(ah-SAH...)
Meat, us...
roasted ...
over a f...

MATE
(MAH-tay)
Mate is a bitter, greenish tea. It is sipped through a silver straw called a bombilla (bome-BEE-yah) from a hollow gourd that is passed around.

FACÓN
(fah-KONE)
A gaucho knife. Gauchos used to carry them as weapons, but now they are used for ranch work.

GAUCHO CLOTHES

BOLEADORAS
(boh-lay-ah-DOOR-ahs)
Gauchos used to catch ñandús and other animals with boleadoras, which they threw in such a way that the animals' legs were tangled up in them.

RASTRA
(RAH-stra)
A gaucho belt made from a wide strip of leather decorated with silver coins, usually from different countries. Some gauchos have their initials on the buckle.

BOMBACHA
(bome-BAH-cha)
Loose gaucho pants.

ÑANDÚ
(nyon-DOO)
The ñandú, or South American ostrich, is the largest bird in the Americas. It grows to be five feet tall and to weigh about fifty pounds. Although it cannot fly, it can run very fast. The male ñandú guards the nest, hatches the eggs, and takes care of the chicks.

RECADO
(ray-KAH-doh)
The gaucho saddle, made of many layers of leather and wool, with a sheepskin on the top.

ESTANCIA
(eh-STAHN-see-ah)
A South American cattle ranch.

ON THE PAMPAS

María Cristina Brusca

Henry Holt and Company
New York

First edition
Published by Henry Holt and Company, Inc.,
115 West 18th Street, New York, New York 10011.
Published simultaneously in Canada by Fitzhenry & Whiteside Limited,
195 Allstate Parkway, Markham, Ontario L3R 4T8.

Library of Congress Cataloging-in-Publication Data
Brusca, María Cristina.
On the pampas / by María Cristina Brusca.
Summary: An account of a little girl's idyllic summer at her
grandparents' ranch on the pampas of Argentina.
ISBN 0-8050-1548-5 (acid-free paper)
1. Pampas (Argentina)—Description and travel—Juvenile
literature.   2. Gauchos—Argentina—Juvenile literature.   3. Ranch
life—Argentina—Juvenile literature.   [1. Pampas (Argentina)—
Description and travel.   2. Argentina—Social life and customs.
3. Gauchos.   4. Ranch life—Argentina.]   I. Title.
F2926.B78   1991
982—dc20   90-40938

Henry Holt books are available at special discounts
for bulk purchases for sales promotions, premiums,
fund-raising, or educational use. Special editions
or book excerpts can also be created to specification.

Printed in the United States of America
on acid-free paper. ∞

1   3   5   7   9   10   8   6   4   2

*To my grandparents María Carlota Rossi
and Hector Pedro Mazza,
and to my cousin Susanita of course*

I grew up in Argentina, in South America. I lived with my family in the big city of Buenos Aires, but we spent our summers in the country, at my grandparents' *estancia*. One summer my parents and brother stayed in the city, so I went without them.

My grandmother met me at the station in Buenos Aires, and we had breakfast as we rode through miles and miles of the flattest land in the world—the pampas. All around us, as far as we could see, were fences, windmills, and millions of cattle grazing.

Our station, San Enrique, was at the end of the line, where the train tracks stopped. My grandfather was there to meet us in his pickup truck and take us the five miles to the estancia.

The ranch was called La Carlota, and the gates were made of iron bars from a fort that had been on that very spot a hundred years before. As we drove up to the gates, we were greeted by a cloud of dust and a thundering of hooves—it was my cousin Susanita, on her horse.

Susanita lived at the estancia all year round. She knew everything about horses, cows, and all the other animals that live on
the pampas. Even though she was three years younger than me,
she had her own horse, La Baya. Susanita was so tiny, she had to
shimmy up La Baya's leg to get on her back. But she rode so well
that the gauchos called her La Gauchita—"The Little Gaucho."

I didn't have a horse of my own, but old Salguero, the ranch foreman, brought me Pampita, a sweet-tempered mare, to ride. She wasn't very fast, but she certainly was my friend.

Susanita and I did everything together that summer. She was the one who showed me how to take care of the horses. We would brush their coats, trim their hooves, and braid their manes and tails.

Susanita was always ready for an adventure, no matter how scary. She used to swim in the creek holding on to La Baya's mane. At first I was afraid to follow her, but when she finally convinced me, it was a lot of fun.

I wanted to learn all the things a gaucho has to know. I wanted to ride out on the pampas every day, as Salguero did, and to wear

a belt like his, with silver coins from all over the world and a
buckle with my initials on it. Salguero said I'd have to begin at the
beginning, and he spent hours showing Susanita and me how to
use the lasso.

It was going to take a while for me to become a gaucho. The first time I lassoed a calf, it dragged me halfway across the corral. But Salguero told me that even he had been dragged plenty of times, so I kept trying, until I got pretty good at it.

Whenever the gauchos were working with the cattle, Susanita was there, and before long I was too. Sometimes the herd had to be rounded up and moved from one pasture to another. I loved galloping behind hundreds of cattle, yelling to make them run. I never got to yell like that in the city!

One day we separated the calves from the cows, to vaccinate them and brand them with "the scissors," La Carlota's mark. That was more difficult—and more exciting, too. I tried to do what Salguero told me to, but sometimes I got lost in the middle of that sea of cattle.

At noon, everybody would sit down around one big table and eat together. I was always hungry. Grandma, Susanita's mother, and Maria the cook had been working hard all morning too. They would make soup, salad, and lamb stew or pot roast, or my favorite, *carbonada*, a thick stew made of corn and peaches.

After lunch the grown-ups took a *siesta*, but not us. We liked
to stay outdoors. Some afternoons, when it was too hot to do
anything else, we rode out to a eucalyptus grove that was nice
and cool, and stayed there until it got dark, reading comic books
or cowboy stories.

Other times we would gallop for two hours to the general store and buy ourselves an orange soda. Then, while we drank it, we'd look at all the saddles and bridles we planned to have when we were grown up and rich. Sometimes the storekeeper would take down a wonderful gaucho belt like Salguero's, and we would admire the silver coins and wonder where each one came from.

One day we rode far away from the house, to a field where
Susanita thought we might find *ñandú* eggs. They are so huge,
you can bake a whole cake with just one of them. After riding
around all afternoon, we found a nest, well hidden in the tall
grass, with about twenty pale-yellow eggs as big as coconuts.

Salguero had warned us to watch out for the ñandú, and he was right! The father ñandú, who protects the nest, saw us taking an egg. He was furious and chased us out of the field.

The next day we used the ñandú egg to bake a birthday cake for my grandmother. We snuck into the kitchen while she was taking her siesta, so it would be a surprise. The cake had three layers, and in between them we put whipped cream and peaches from the trees on the ranch.

We had a wonderful party for my grandmother's birthday. The gauchos started the fire for the *asado* early in the evening, and soon the smell of the slowly cooking meat filled the air.

There was music, and dancing, too. We stayed up almost all night, and I learned to dance the *zamba*, taking little steps and hops, and twirling my handkerchief.

Most evenings were much quieter. There was just the hum of the generator that made electricity for the house. We liked to go out to the *mate* house, where the gauchos spent their evenings.

We listened to them tell ghost stories and tall tales while they sat around the fire, passing the gourd and sipping mate through the silver straw. We didn't like the hot, bitter tea, but we loved being frightened by their spooky stories.

The summer was drawing to a close, and soon I would be returning to Buenos Aires. The night before I was to leave, Salguero showed me how to find the Southern Cross. The generator had been turned off, and there was only the soft sound of the peepers. We could see the horses sleeping far off in the field.

The next morning, my last at the estancia, Susanita and I got
up before dawn. Pampita and the other horses were still out in
the field. Salguero handed me his own horse's reins. He told me
he thought I was ready to bring in the horses by myself. I wasn't
sure I could do it, but Susanita encouraged me to try.

I remembered what I'd seen Salguero do. I tried to get the leading mare, with her bell, to go toward the corral, and the others would follow her. It wasn't easy. The foals were frisky and kept running away. But I stayed behind them until finally the little herd was all together, trotting in front of me.

I was so busy trying to keep the foals from running off that I didn't notice the whole household waiting in the corral with Salguero. Everyone cheered as I rode in, and before I knew it, my grandfather was helping me off the horse. "You've become quite a gaucho this summer," he said. My grandmother held out a wonderful gaucho belt like Salguero's, with silver coins from around the world—and my initials on the buckle!

"And," she added, "there's something else every gaucho needs. Next summer, when you come back, you'll have your very own horse waiting for you!" She pointed to the leading mare's foal, the friskiest and most beautiful of them all.

Before I could say a word, the foal pranced over to me, tossing his head. I would have the whole winter to decide what to name him, and to look forward to my next summer on the pampas.

MULITA

(moo-LEE-ta)
The mulita is a kind of armadillo. It spends the day in its burrow and comes out at night to look for food, mostly spiders and insects.

LAS PAMPAS

(las POM-pas)
The pampas are the very flat, almost treeless grasslands that stretch for hundreds of miles through central Argentina and Uruguay. Ranch animals live on the pampas year round, even during the mild winter months, eating grass.

HORNERO
(or-NAIR-oh)
The hornero is a kind of oven bird. Its nest looks something like an oven and is built out of clay, usually on top of a post or pole.

REBENQUE

(ray-BAIN-kay)
A short, wide rawhide strap, used to lash cattle and horses.

LA CARLOTA'S BRAND

(la car-LOH-ta)
The brand represented two cross fencing swords, but we called the "the scissors."

LECHUZA

(lay-CHOO-sa)
The lechuza, or burrowing owl, makes its home in holes abandoned by armadillos or other mammals. It likes to hunt in the evening.

YEGUA MADRINA

(YAY-goo-ah mah-DREE-na)
The yegua madrina, or leading mare of a herd of horses, keeps the herd together. She generally has a bell around her neck.

VENEZUELA
COLOMBIA
GUYANA
SURINAME
FRENCH GUIANA
ECUADOR
SOUTH AMERICA
PERÚ
BRAZIL
BOLIVIA
PARAGUAY
ARGENTINA
CHILE
THE PAMPAS
URUGUAY
BUENOS AIRES
LA CARLOTA
SOUTH PACIFIC OCEAN
SOUTH ATLANTIC OCEAN